Bread of Life

RSCM Young Voices Festival

The Royal School of Church Music
19 The Close, Salisbury, Wiltshire, SPI 2EB

The Royal School of Church Music
19 The Close, Salisbury, Wiltshire SP1 2EB
E-mail: education@rscm.com Website: www.rscm.com

Bread of Life
RSCM Young Voices Festival

RSCM Order Code: S0143
RSCM Catalogue Number: RS44
ISBN: 978-0-85402-196-3

Service devised by Dr Michael O'Connor
with thanks to the Revd James Steven and Ian Wicks
Cover design by Anthony Marks
Music and text origination by RSCM Press
Printed in Great Britain by Caligraving Ltd

CD recorded by The Bishop's Singers, Salisbury
Directed by Ian Wicks
Piano played by Matthew Jorysz
Recording by Vif Records

Contents

Part I: Conductor's Score

I–Gathering

II–The heavenly banquet

III–Harvest for the hungry

IV–I am the living bread

V–Sending out

Part II: Singers' Music

I–Gathering

II–The heavenly Banquet

III–Harvest for the hungry

IV–I am the living bread

V–Sending out

Copyright and Acknowledgements

Introduction

The Royal School of Church Music Young Voices Festival is an opportunity for young people from schools and churches to join together in song in fabulous venues across the UK. It offers an inspiring musical and spiritual experience for all participants, and a chance to develop vocal and musical skills under expert musical direction.

The festival is a *Voice for Life* outreach event. The *Voice for Life* scheme is one of the RSCM's core educational programmes, which exists to encourage, support and promote singing in schools, churches and the wider community.

This book and CD-ROM contain everything you and your singers need to participate in the service.

The book contains:

The conductor's score. This contains the entire service, including readings, prayers and full music scores. This part of the book may not be photocopied.

The singers' music. You may photocopy these pages to give to your singers.

The singers' music is also available on the CD-ROM so you can print this out as a booklet from your computer.

The CD-ROM contains resources that you can print from your computer, and includes:

- The readings
- The singers' music booklet
- The order of service which you can print off for the congregation
- Training notes for all the anthems

If you are using the *Bread of Life* festival locally, please feel free to treat the service flexibly and incorporate your own creative ideas. You may also like to use individual items in your services, concert programmes or assemblies.

Guidance on how to arrange your own Young Voices Festival can be found on the RSCM website at: www.rscm.com/education/youngvoicesfestival.php

We hope you enjoy *Bread of Life*.

Bread of Life

RSCM Young Voices Festival

The following pages may NOT be photocopied

RSCM

The Royal School of Church Music
19 The Close, Salisbury, Wiltshire, SP1 2EB

GATHERING

 CD: Track 1 complete performance

Gathering song: **Wa wa wa Emimimo** *Singers' music booklet page II:2*

Music: Nigerian
arranged by Geoff Weaver

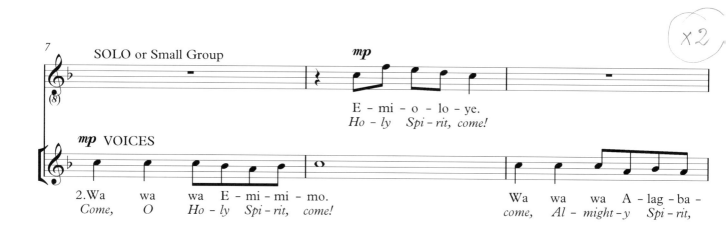

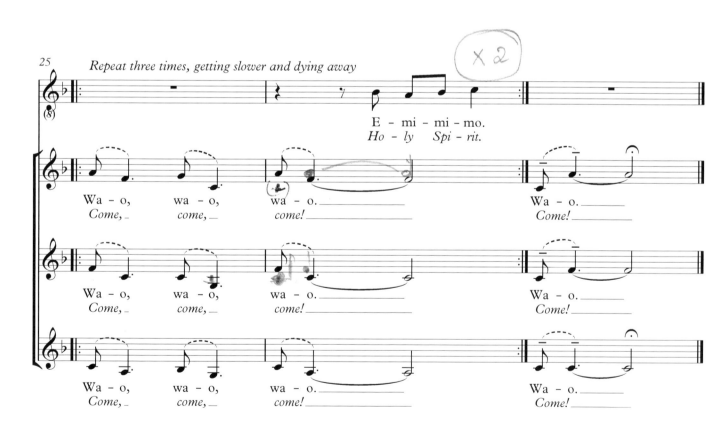

I – THE HEAVENLY BANQUET

Responsory and greeting

The Lord has chosen Zion for himself;
All   he has desired it for his dwelling.

On my holy mountain, I will satisfy my people with bread.
All   The poor shall rejoice and sing.

Psalm 132.14–15

Pilgrims journeying towards the heavenly city,
we have gathered in the name of Christ
and at the inspiration of the Holy Spirit
to pray and praise the Father of all goodness:
All   Blessed be God who gives us bread from heaven.

CD: Track 2 complete performance, **Track 10** piano accompaniment

Hymn: Lord, enthroned in heavenly splendour *Singers' music booklet page 11:6*

Words: George Bourne 1840–1925

Music: G. C. Martin 1844–1916
Last verse arrangement & descant: Lindsay Gray

ST. HELEN

1. Lord en - throned in heaven - ly splen-dour first - be - gott - en from the dead,
2. Here our humb-lest ho - mage pay we, here in lo - ving rev - erence bow;
3. Pas - chal Lamb, thine off - ering, fin - ished once for all when thou wast slain,

thou a - lone, our strong de - fend - er lift - est up thy peo - ple's head.
here for faith's dis - cern - ment pray we, lest we fail to know thee now.
in its full - ness un - di - min - ished shall for ev - er - more re - main,

Al - le - lu - ia, al - le - lu - ia, Je - su true and li - ving bread.
Al - le - lu - ia, al - le - lu - ia, thou art here, we ask not how.
Al - le - lu - ia, al - le - lu - ia, cleans - ing souls from ev - ery stain.

Reading
Exodus 16:11–15

Manna from Heaven

The Lord said to Moses,
> 'I have heard the complaints of the Israelites. Tell them that at twilight they will have meat to eat, and in the morning they will have all the bread they want. Then they will know that I, the Lord, am their God.'

In the evening a large flock of quails flew in, enough to cover the camp, and in the morning there was dew all around the camp. When the dew evaporated, there was something thin and flaky on the surface of the desert. It was as delicate as frost. When the Israelites saw it, they didn't know what it was and asked each other,
> 'What is it?'

Moses said to them,
> 'This is the food that the Lord has given you to eat.'

CD: Track 3 complete performance, **Track 11** piano accompaniment

Anthem: Panis angelicus *Singers' music booklet page II:8*

Latin Text: Thomas Aquinas (1227–1274)
English Text: David Patrick

César Franck (1822–1890)
edited and arranged by David Patrick

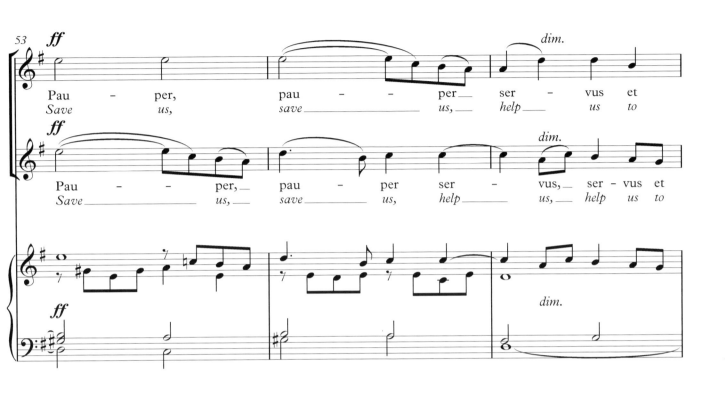

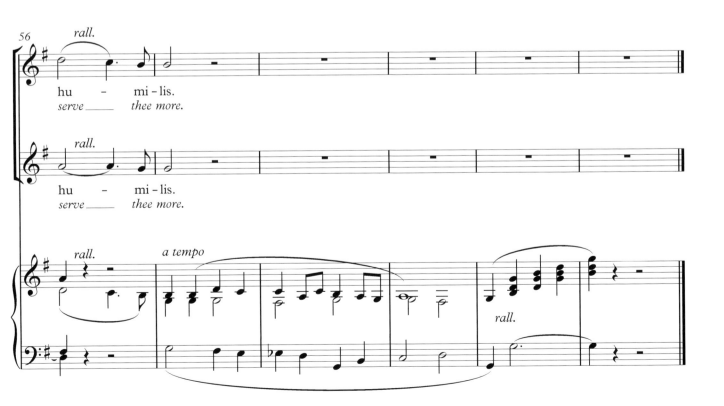

Reading

From the visions of Julian of Norwich (c. 1342–after 1413)

And in this vision my understanding was lifted up into heaven.
There I saw our Lord, the master in his own house.
He had called all his cherished servants and friends to a stately feast.
Then I saw the Lord take no place in his own house,
but I saw him royally reign in his house,
filling it full with joy and mirth,
himself endlessly to gladden and to comfort his cherished friends,
full homely and full courteously.
In his own fair blessed face was a marvellous melody of endless love.
This glorious face of the Godhead fills the heavens to overflowing with joy and bliss.

Prayer

Lord Jesus,
a table of food stands at the centre of the life you promise,
a table to which all are invited, of every race and nation;
a table at which you are host and servant;
a table of unity and love.
You have filled us with a hunger for this heavenly banquet;
Help us to live now its fellowship on earth.

All   Amen.

CD: Track 4 complete performance, **Track 12** piano accompaniment

Prayer response: Bread of life *Singers' music booklet page II:10*

Words & Music: Bernadette Farrell

Slow, with serenity

III   HARVEST FOR THE HUNGRY

Responsory

All your creatures look to you, O Lord.
All   You give them their food in due season.

You give it them, they gather it up;
All   you open your hands and they are filled with good things.

You hide your face, they are brought to confusion.
All   You take away their breath, they return to the dust.

When you send forth your spirit, they are created,
All   and you renew the face of the earth.

CD: Track 5 complete performance, **Track 13** piano accompaniment

Song: Beauty for brokenness *Singers' music booklet page II:12*

Words: Graham Kendrick

Music: Graham Kendrick
arranged John Barnard

from a spark _____ to a ____ flame.

love _____ from a spark to a flame.

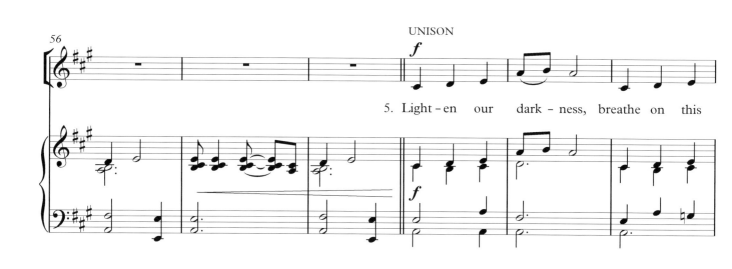

UNISON

5. Light-en our dark-ness, breathe on this

flame _____ un-til your jus-tice burns bright-ly a-gain; un-til the na-tions

learn of your ways, seek your sal - va - tion and bring you their praise.

DESCANT
God of the poor, friend of the weak,

ALL OTHER VOICES
God of the poor,___ friend of the weak,___

give us com - pas - sion, we pray. Melt our cold hearts, let

give us com - pas - sion, we pray. Melt our cold hearts, let

tears   fall   like   rain.   Come,   change   our   love

tears   fall   like   rain.   Come,   change   our   love   from   a

from   a   spark   to   a   flame.

spark   to   a   flame.

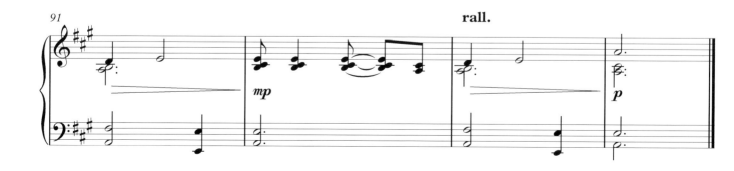

Reading

Isaiah 58:6–9a

True fasting

The kind of fasting I want is this: Remove the chains of oppression and the yoke of injustice, and let the oppressed go free. Share your food with the hungry and open your homes to the homeless poor. Give clothes to those who have nothing to wear, and do not refuse to help your own relatives.

Then my favour will shine on you like the morning sun, and your wounds will be quickly healed. I will always be with you to save you; my presence will protect you on every side. When you pray, I will answer you. When you call to me, I will respond.

CD: Track 6 complete performance, **Track 14** piano accompaniment

Anthem: The bread of the hungry *Singers' music booklet page II:16*

Words: St Basil the Great

Music: Thomas Hewitt Jones

The mo - ney you keep locked a - way

The mo - ney you keep locked a - way

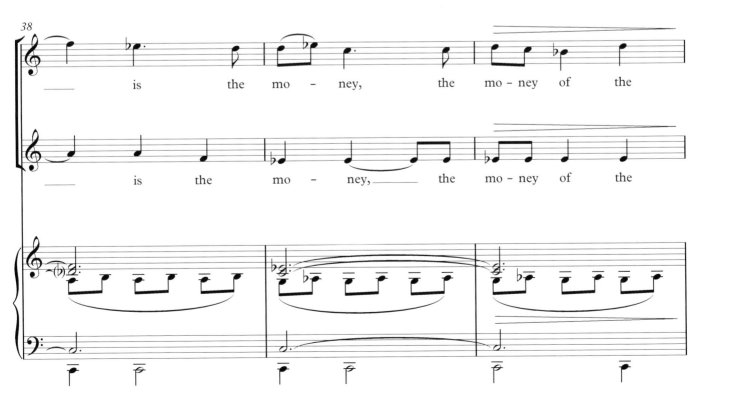

is the mo - ney, the mo - ney of the

is the mo - ney, the mo - ney of the

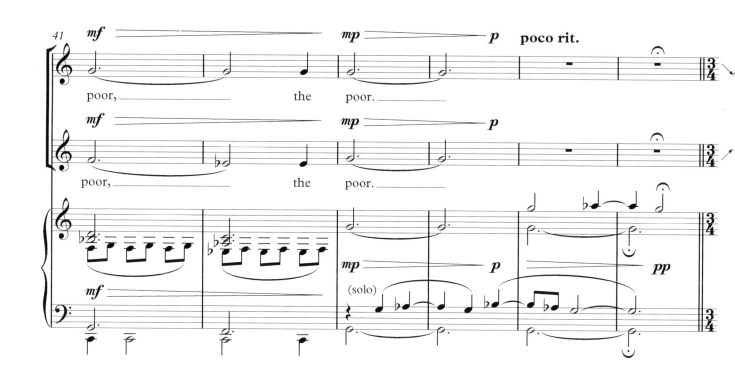

Reading
From the little flowers of St Francis of Assisi

There were three robbers who terrified the district where St Francis and his friars lived. One day they came to the friary and asked Brother Angelo to give them bread. Brother Angelo spoke to them harshly:

'You shameless thieves and murderers! You steal from others the bread they have sweated hard to earn. And now you have the cheek to ask us, God's poor servants, for the food we have begged? Be gone! And do not dare to show your faces around here again.'

Dumbfounded by these words, the robbers slunk away, embarrassed.

By and by, St Francis returned to the friary with a sack of bread and a jug of wine that he and his companions had begged in a neighbouring village. When Brother Angelo proudly told how he had sent the thieves packing, Francis scolded him:

'Angelo, you should lead people to God with gentleness not cruelty. Do you not remember what Jesus taught us? It is not the healthy who need the doctor, but the sick. Our master did not come to call the just, but sinners to repentance. He was not ashamed to eat with sinners and to be found in the company of outcasts.'

Brother Angelo was crestfallen. Francis continued, 'This is what you must do to amend for your lack of kindness: take this sack of bread and jug of wine. Go into the hills, after those thieves, and do not stop until you have found them. Give them the bread and the wine, from me. Then fall down on your knees and ask for forgiveness. When you have done this, ask them, on my account, to do no more evil, but to fear God and serve their neighbour. And if they do this, I promise that they will have food and drink from me always.'

Brother Angelo set off as instructed, less sure than before, and praying fervently that God would soften the hearts of the thieves. When he found them, he gave them the bread and the wine, and said and did all that Francis had asked him. Hearing his words, and taking the food and drink he had brought, they were cut to the quick:

'We are wicked men, violent and murderous, without conscience before God. But this friar has asked forgiveness for his sharp words to us – which were no more than we deserved. And he has brought food for our hungry bellies. Holy friar, what must we do?

Brother Angelo brought them to Francis who welcomed them gently. He comforted them with many examples of the great mercy of God. He promised to beg God's mercy for them, and he showed them that the mercy of God is infinite. And they repented of their sins, did penance, and began to walk in the ways of the Lord.

Prayer

Almighty God,
the world turns at your command:
day and night, month and season, seedtime and harvest.
But the stomachs of the poor are empty,
and the mouths of the hungry cry out against injustice.
Bend our wills, and make us faithful stewards of fruits of the land:
Pull down our bigger barns and confound our greed.
Where hunger is greatest, may we be most generous.

All   Amen.

CD: Track 4 complete performance, **Track 12** piano accompaniment

Prayer response: Bread of life *Singers' music booklet page II:20*

Words & Music: Bernadette Farrell

Slow, with serenity

Bread of life, hope of the world, Je-sus Christ, our bro-ther: feed us now, give us life, lead us to one an-oth-er.

final time

IV I AM THE LIVING BREAD

Responsory

He led them with a pillar of cloud by day
All   **and all night with a pillar of fire.**

He split the hard rocks in the wilderness and gave them drink from the depths.
All   **He commanded the clouds above and opened the doors of heaven.**

In the wilderness, God rained down manna to eat;
He gave them the grain of heaven, they had food in plenty.
All   **So mortals ate the bread of angels.**

Psalm 78.14–15,23–25

CD: Track 7 complete performance, **Track 15** piano accompaniment

Hymn: Christ be our light! *Singers' music booklet page II:22*

Words and Music: Bernadette Farrell (b.1957)

Refrain

Reading

John 6:8–14, 35

The bread of life

Narrator   One of Jesus' disciples, Andrew, who was Simon Peter's brother, said:

Andrew   There is a boy here who has five loaves of barley bread and two fish. But they will certainly not be enough for all these people.

Jesus   Make the people sit down.

Narrator   There was a lot of grass there. So all the people sat down; there were about five thousand men. Jesus took the bread, gave thanks to God, and distributed it to the people who were sitting there. He did the same with the fish, and they all had as much as they wanted. When they were all full, he said to his disciples:

Jesus   Gather the pieces left over; let us not waste any.

Narrator   So they gathered them all and filled twelve baskets with the pieces left over from the five barley loaves which the people had eaten.

(Pause)

Seeing this miracle that Jesus had performed, the people there said:

Persons 1&2   Surely this is the Prophet who was to come into the world!

Jesus   I am the bread of life. Those who come to me will never be hungry; those who believe in me will never be thirsty.'

Prayer

Lord Jesus, you fed the hungry crowds,
and you feed us with the bread of life:
Through the gift of yourself
help us to become more like you

All   Amen.

member of staff.

CD: Track 8 complete performance, **Track 16** piano accompaniment

Anthem: I am the bread of life *Singers' music booklet page II:25*

Words: John 6: 35

Music: Simon Lole
(b. 1957)

Reading

From a hymn of Ephraim of Edessa

In your bread is hidden the unconsumable Spirit,
In your wine dwells the undrinkable fire.
Spirit in your bread, fire in your wine,
A wonder from on high, received by our lips!

Fire and Spirit in the womb that bore you.
Fire and Spirit in the river where you were baptized.
Fire and Spirit in our baptism;
In the bread and the cup, fire and Holy Spirit!

Your bread kills death, who had made us his bread,
Your cup destroys the devourer, which was swallowing us up.
We have eaten you, Lord, we have drunk you,
Not to exhaust you, but to live by you.

Prayer

Gracious Jesus,
Make us know that hunger that is within us—
but be to us the bread that satisfies;
Place upon us any burden—
but strengthen us with pilgrims' food;
Show us the faces of the hungry and the poor—
but be the bread in our hands that we share with them.
For you are the way, the truth and the life—
to whom else can we go but you?

All   Amen

CD: Track 4 complete performance, **Track 12** piano accompaniment

Prayer response *Singers' music booklet page II:28*

Words & Music: Bernadette Farrell

Slow, with serenity

Bread of life, hope of the world,
Je‑sus Christ, our bro‑ther: feed us now, give us life,
lead us to one an‑oth‑er.

Prayers

Let us pray to God our creator,
who has given us the earth's goodness for our delight,
and entrusted it to our care and tenderness.

For all who live in captivity to debt,
whose lives are cramped by fear
from which there is no turning
except through abundant harvest;
Lord, we pray: may those who sow in tears

All   reap with shouts of joy.

For all who depend on the earth for their daily food and fuel,
whose forests are destroyed for the profit of a few;
Lord, we pray: may those who sow in tears

All   reap with shouts of joy.

For those who labour in poverty,
are oppressed by unjust laws,
are prevented from speaking the truth,
and long for a harvest of justice;
Lord we pray: may those who sow in tears

All   reap with shouts of joy.

For all who are captive to greed and waste and boredom,
whose harvest joy is choked with things they do not need;
Lord, we pray: may those who sow in tears

All   reap with shouts of joy.

O God,
your Son made himself known to his disciples in
        the breaking of bread:
open the eyes of our faith,
that we may see him in his redeeming work

All   Amen.

The Lord's Prayer

Gathering all our prayers and offerings into one,
as our Saviour has taught us, so we pray

All   **Our Father in heaven,**
hallowed be your name,
your kingdom come,
your will be done,
on earth as in heaven.
Give us today our daily bread.
Forgive us our sins
as we forgive those who sin against us.
Lead us not into temptation
but deliver us from evil.
For the kingdom, the power,
and the glory are yours
now and for ever.
Amen.

V SENDING OUT

 CD: Track 9 complete performance, **Track 17** piano accompaniment

Hymn: Guide me, O thou great Redeemer *Singers' music booklet page II:31*

Words: William Williams 1717–1791
tr. Peter & William Williams

Music: John Hughes 1873–1932
last verse descant: Malcolm Archer b.1952

Bread   of   hea - ven,   bread   of   hea - ven,   feed   me   now   and   e - ver-
strong   de - live - rer,   strong   de - live - rer,   be   thou   still   my   strength   and

more,   feed   me   now___   and___   e - ver - more.
shield,   be   thou   still___   my___   strength   and   shield.

LAST VERSE DESCANT

3. When   I   tread   the   verge_   of___   Jor - dan,   bid   my_   an - xious   fears   sub - side;

ALL OTHER VOICES

3. When   I   tread   the   verge_   of___   Jor - dan,   bid   my   an - xious   fears   sub - side;

Blessing

May God the Father of our Lord Jesus Christ,
who is the source of all goodness and growth,
pour his blessing upon on things created,
and upon you his children,
that you may use his gifts to his glory
and the welfare of all peoples;
and the blessing of God almighty,
the Father, the Son, and the Holy Spirit,
be among you and remain with you always

All   Amen

Dismissal

Tend the earth, care for God's good creation,
and bring forth the fruits of righteousness.
Go in the peace of Christ.

All   Thanks be to God.

Bread of Life

RSCM Young Voices Festival

The following pages MAY be photocopied for your singers

The Royal School of Church Music
19 The Close, Salisbury, Wiltshire, SP1 2EB

GATHERING

Gathering song: Wa wa wa Emimimo

Music: Nigerian
arranged by Geoff Weaver

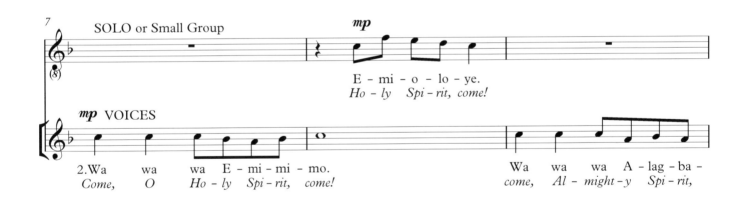

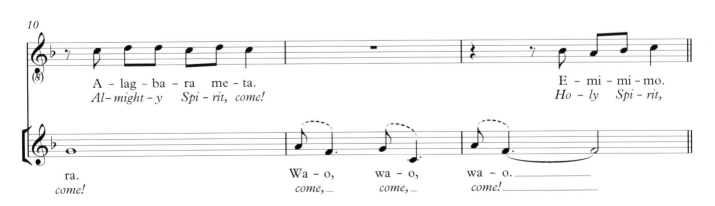

I – THE HEAVENLY BANQUET

Responsory and greeting

The Lord has chosen Zion for himself;

All   **he has desired it for his dwelling.**

On my holy mountain, I will satisfy my people with bread.

All   **The poor shall rejoice and sing.**

Psalm 132.14–15

Pilgrims journeying towards the heavenly city,
we have gathered in the name of Christ
and at the inspiration of the Holy Spirit
to pray and praise the Father of all goodness:

All   **Blessed be God who gives us bread from heaven.**

Hymn: Lord, enthroned in heavenly splendour

Words: George Bourne 1840–1925

Music: G. C. Martin 1844–1916
Last verse arrangement & descant: Lindsay Gray

Reading
Exodus 16:11–15

Manna from Heaven

The Lord said to Moses,

> 'I have heard the complaints of the Israelites. Tell them that at twilight they will have meat to eat, and in the morning they will have all the bread they want. Then they will know that I, the Lord, am their God.'

In the evening a large flock of quails flew in, enough to cover the camp, and in the morning there was dew all around the camp. When the dew evaporated, there was something thin and flaky on the surface of the desert. It was as delicate as frost. When the Israelites saw it, they didn't know what it was and asked each other,

> 'What is it?'

Moses said to them,

> 'This is the food that the Lord has given you to eat.'

Anthem: Panis angelicus

Latin Text: Thomas Aquinas (1227–1274)
English Text: David Patrick

César Franck (1822–1890)
edited and arranged by David Patrick

Reading

From the visions of Julian of Norwich (c. 1342–after 1413)

And in this vision my understanding was lifted up into heaven.

There I saw our Lord, the master in his own house.

He had called all his cherished servants and friends to a stately feast.

Then I saw the Lord take no place in his own house,

but I saw him royally reign in his house,

filling it full with joy and mirth,

himself endlessly to gladden and to comfort his cherished friends,

full homely and full courteously.

In his own fair blessed face was a marvellous melody of endless love.

This glorious face of the Godhead fills the heavens to overflowing with joy and bliss.

Prayer

Lord Jesus,

a table of food stands at the centre of the life you promise,

a table to which all are invited, of every race and nation;

a table at which you are host and servant;

a table of unity and love.

You have filled us with a hunger for this heavenly banquet;

Help us to live now its fellowship on earth.

All   Amen.

Prayer response: Bread of life

Words & Music: Bernadette Farrell

Slow, with serenity

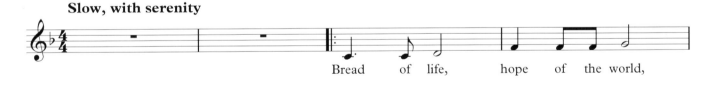

Bread of life, hope of the world,

Je - sus Christ, our bro - ther: feed us now, give us life,

final time

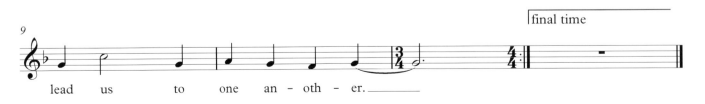

lead us to one an - oth - er.

III HARVEST FOR THE HUNGRY

Responsory

All your creatures look to you, O Lord.
All   **You give them their food in due season.**

You give it them, they gather it up;
All   **you open your hands and they are filled with good things.**

You hide your face, they are brought to confusion.
All   **You take away their breath, they return to the dust.**

When you send forth your spirit, they are created,
All   **and you renew the face of the earth.**

Song: Beauty for brokenness

Words: Graham Kendrick

Music: Graham Kendrick
arranged John Barnard

God of the poor, — friend of the weak, — give us com - pas -

God of the poor, friend of the weak, give us com -

- sion, we pray. Melt our cold hearts, let tears fall like — rain.

pas - sion, we pray. Melt our cold hearts, let tears fall like rain.

Come, change our love — from a spark — to a — flame.

Come, change our love — from a spark to a flame.

5. Light - en our dark - ness, breathe on this flame

un - til your jus - tice burns bright - ly a - gain; un - til the na - tions

learn of your ways, seek your sal - va - tion and bring you their praise.

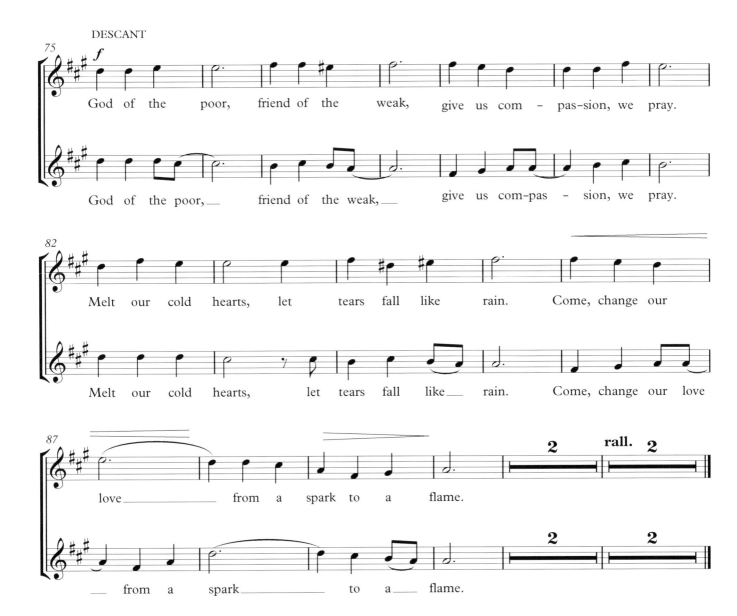

Reading

Isaiah 58:6–9a

True fasting

The kind of fasting I want is this: Remove the chains of oppression and the yoke of injustice, and let the oppressed go free. Share your food with the hungry and open your homes to the homeless poor. Give clothes to those who have nothing to wear, and do not refuse to help your own relatives.

Then my favour will shine on you like the morning sun, and your wounds will be quickly healed. I will always be with you to save you; my presence will protect you on every side. When you pray, I will answer you. When you call to me, I will respond.

Anthem: The bread of the hungry

Words: St Basil the Great

Music: Thomas Hewitt Jones

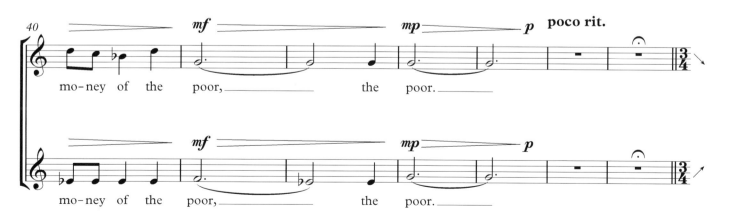

Reading

From the little flowers of St Francis of Assisi

There were three robbers who terrified the district where St Francis and his friars lived. One day they came to the friary and asked Brother Angelo to give them bread. Brother Angelo spoke to them harshly:

'You shameless thieves and murderers! You steal from others the bread they have sweated hard to earn. And now you have the cheek to ask us, God's poor servants, for the food we have begged? Be gone! And do not dare to show your faces around here again.'

Dumbfounded by these words, the robbers slunk away, embarrassed.

By and by, St Francis returned to the friary with a sack of bread and a jug of wine that he and his companions had begged in a neighbouring village. When Brother Angelo proudly told how he had sent the thieves packing, Francis scolded him:

'Angelo, you should lead people to God with gentleness not cruelty. Do you not remember what Jesus taught us? It is not the healthy who need the doctor, but the sick. Our master did not come to call the just, but sinners to repentance. He was not ashamed to eat with sinners and to be found in the company of outcasts.'

Brother Angelo was crestfallen. Francis continued, 'This is what you must do to amend for your lack of kindness: take this sack of bread and jug of wine. Go into the hills, after those thieves, and do not stop until you have found them. Give them the bread and the wine, from me. Then fall down on your knees and ask for forgiveness. When you have done this, ask them, on my account, to do no more evil, but to fear God and serve their neighbour. And if they do this, I promise that they will have food and drink from me always.'

Brother Angelo set off as instructed, less sure than before, and praying fervently that God would soften the hearts of the thieves. When he found them, he gave them the bread and the wine, and said and did all that Francis had asked him. Hearing his words, and taking the food and drink he had brought, they were cut to the quick:

'We are wicked men, violent and murderous, without conscience before God. But this friar has asked forgiveness for his sharp words to us – which were no more than we deserved. And he has brought food for our hungry bellies. Holy friar, what must we do?

Brother Angelo brought them to Francis who welcomed them gently. He comforted them with many examples of the great mercy of God. He promised to beg God's mercy for them, and he showed them that the mercy of God is infinite. And they repented of their sins, did penance, and began to walk in the ways of the Lord.

Prayer

Almighty God,
the world turns at your command:
day and night, month and season, seedtime and harvest.
But the stomachs of the poor are empty,
and the mouths of the hungry cry out against injustice.
Bend our wills, and make us faithful stewards of fruits of the land:
Pull down our bigger barns and confound our greed.
Where hunger is greatest, may we be most generous.

All   Amen.

Prayer response: Bread of life

Words & Music: Bernadette Farrell

Slow, with serenity

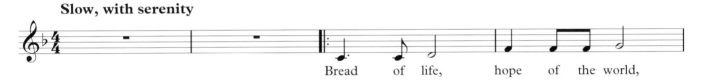

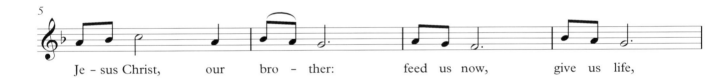

IV I AM THE LIVING BREAD

Responsory

He led them with a pillar of cloud by day
All   and all night with a pillar of fire.

He split the hard rocks in the wilderness and gave them drink from the depths.
All   He commanded the clouds above and opened the doors of heaven.

In the wilderness, God rained down manna to eat;
He gave them the grain of heaven, they had food in plenty.
All   So mortals ate the bread of angels.

Psalm 78.14–15,23–25

Hymn: Christ be our light!

Words and Music: Bernadette Farrell (b.1957)

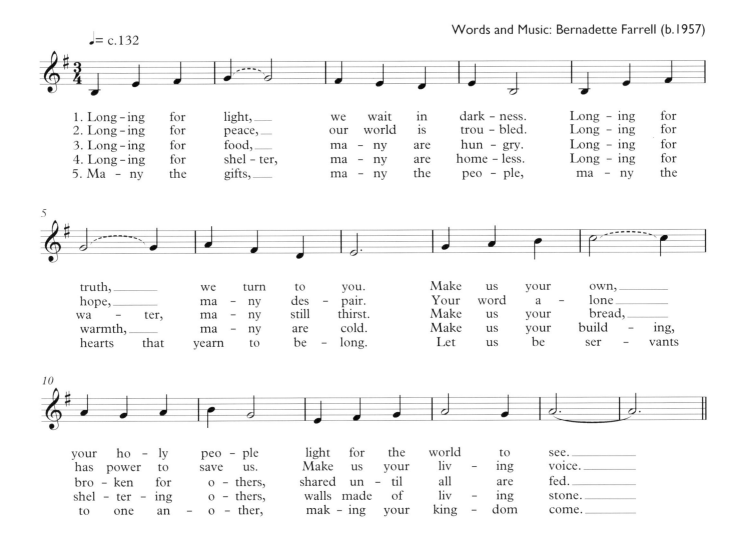

♩= c.132

1. Long-ing for light,___ we wait in dark-ness. Long-ing for
2. Long-ing for peace,___ our world is trou-bled. Long-ing for
3. Long-ing for food,___ ma - ny are hun-gry. Long-ing for
4. Long-ing for shel-ter, ma - ny are home-less. Long-ing for
5. Ma - ny the gifts,___ ma - ny the peo - ple, ma - ny the

truth,___ we turn to you. Make us your own,___
hope,___ ma - ny des - pair. Your word a - lone___
wa - ter, ma - ny still thirst. Make us your bread,___
warmth,___ ma - ny are cold. Make us your build - ing,
hearts that yearn to be - long. Let us be ser - vants

your ho - ly peo - ple light for the world to see.___
has power to save us. Make us your liv - ing voice.___
bro - ken for o - thers, shared un - til all are fed.___
shel - ter - ing o - thers, walls made of liv - ing stone.___
to one an - o - ther, mak - ing your king - dom come.___

Refrain

DESCANT *Last verse only*

Christ, be our light! Shine out through the dark, shine!___

Christ, be our light! Shine in our hearts, shine through the dark - ness.

Christ, ____ be our light! Shine in your church gath - ered to -

Christ, be our light! Shine in your church ga - thered to -

To verses | *Last time*

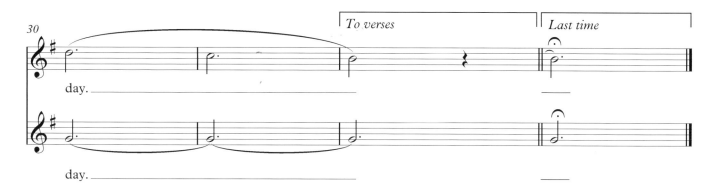

day. _____

day. _____

Reading

John 6:8–14, 35

The bread of life

Narrator   One of Jesus' disciples, Andrew, who was Simon Peter's brother, said:

Andrew   There is a boy here who has five loaves of barley bread and two fish.
But they will certainly not be enough for all these people.

Jesus   Make the people sit down.

Narrator   There was a lot of grass there. So all the people sat down; there were about five thousand men. Jesus took the bread, gave thanks to God, and distributed it to the people who were sitting there. He did the same with the fish, and they all had as much as they wanted. When they were all full, he said to his disciples:

Jesus   Gather the pieces left over; let us not waste any.

Narrator   So they gathered them all and filled twelve baskets with the pieces left over from the five barley loaves which the people had eaten.

(Pause)

Seeing this miracle that Jesus had performed, the people there said:

Persons 1&2   Surely this is the Prophet who was to come into the world!

Jesus   I am the bread of life. Those who come to me will never be hungry;
those who believe in me will never be thirsty.'

Prayer

Lord Jesus, you fed the hungry crowds,
and you feed us with the bread of life:
Through the gift of yourself
help us to become more like you

All   **Amen.**

Anthem: I am the bread of life

Words: John 6: 35

Music: Simon Lole

Reading
From a hymn of Ephraim of Edessa

In your bread is hidden the unconsumable Spirit,
In your wine dwells the undrinkable fire.
Spirit in your bread, fire in your wine,
A wonder from on high, received by our lips!

Fire and Spirit in the womb that bore you.
Fire and Spirit in the river where you were baptized.
Fire and Spirit in our baptism;
In the bread and the cup, fire and Holy Spirit!

Your bread kills death, who had made us his bread,
Your cup destroys the devourer, which was swallowing us up.
We have eaten you, Lord, we have drunk you,
Not to exhaust you, but to live by you.

Prayer

Gracious Jesus,
Make us know that hunger that is within us–
but be to us the bread that satisfies;
Place upon us any burden–
but strengthen us with pilgrims' food;
Show us the faces of the hungry and the poor–
but be the bread in our hands that we share with them.
For you are the way, the truth and the life–
to whom else can we go but you?

All   Amen

Prayer response

Words & Music: Bernadette Farrell

Slow, with serenity

Bread of life, hope of the world,

Je - sus Christ, our bro - ther: feed us now, give us life,

|final time

lead us to one an - oth - er.

Prayers

Let us pray to God our creator,
who has given us the earth's goodness for our delight,
and entrusted it to our care and tenderness.

For all who live in captivity to debt,
whose lieves are cramped by fear
from which there is no turning
except through abundant harvest;
Lord, we pray: may those who sow in tears

All   **reap with shouts of joy.**

For all who depend on the earth for their daily food and fuel,
whose forests are destroyed for the profit of a few;
Lord, we pray: may those who sow in tears

All   **reap with shouts of joy.**

For those who labour in poverty,
are oppressed by unjust laws,
are prevented from speaking the truth,
and long for a harvest of justice;
Lord we pray: may those who sow in tears

All   **reap with shouts of joy.**

For all who are captive to greed and waste and boredom,
whose harvest joy is choked with things they do not need;
Lord, we pray: may those who sow in tears

All   **reap with shouts of joy.**

O God,
your Son made himself known to his disciples in
      the breaking of bread:
open the eyes of our faith,
that we may see him in his redeeming work

All   **Amen.**

The Lord's Prayer

Gathering all our prayers and offerings into one,
as our Saviour has taught us, so we pray

**Our Father in heaven,
hallowed be your name,
your kingdom come,
your will be done,
on earth as in heaven.
Give us today our daily bread.
Forgive us our sins
as we forgive those who sin against us.
Lead us not into temptation
but deliver us from evil.
For the kingdom, the power,
and the glory are yours
now and for ever.
Amen.**

V SENDING OUT

Hymn: Guide me, O thou great Redeemer

Words: William Williams 1717–1791
tr. Peter & William Williams

Music: John Hughes 1873–1932
last verse descant: Malcolm Archer

CWM RHONDDA

1. Guide me, O thou great Re - deem - er, pil - grim through this
2. O - pen now the crys - tal foun - tain whence the heal - ing

bar - ren land; I am weak, but thou art migh - ty;
stream doth flow; let the fie - ry clou - dy pil - lar

hold me with thy pow'r - ful hand: Bread of hea - ven,
lead me all my journ - ey through: strong de - live - rer,

bread of hea - ven, feed me now and e - ver - more,
strong de - live - rer, be thou still my strength and shield,

feed me now and e - ver - more.
be thou still my strength and shield.

Please turn over for last verse

Blessing

May God the Father of our Lord Jesus Christ,
who is the source of all goodness and growth,
pour his blessing upon on things created,
and upon you his children,
that you may use his gifts to his glory
and the welfare of all peoples;
and the blessing of God almighty,
the Father, the Son, and the Holy Spirit,
be among you and remain with you always.

All   **Amen.**

Dismissal

Tend the earth, care for God's good creation,
and bring forth the fruits of righteousness.
Go in the peace of Christ.

All   **Thanks be to God.**